CAMP STUFF

24 PAGE COLORING BOOK

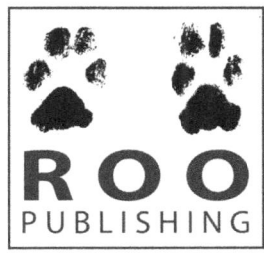

ROO
PUBLISHING

Illustrations by Dani Kates

Dear Colorer,

My name is Dani and I drew the pictures in this coloring book!
I'm an artist, a designer, and a HUGE fan of coloring.
When I buy a coloring book, the first thing I do is take a thin black pen and
draw tiny detailed lines and patterns to make the pictures more fun to color.
I love doing it so much that I decided to design my own coloring books with the
same type of detailed lines and fun patterns.

All of those details and lines make this is an "adult" style coloring book,
but the pictures are way more fun to color!

This one is all about Camp.
Packing for camp, the camp bus, color war, and so much more!

So have fun, color something amazing and share it with me on social media!
@ColorWithDani
#ColorWithDani

XOXO,
Dani Kates

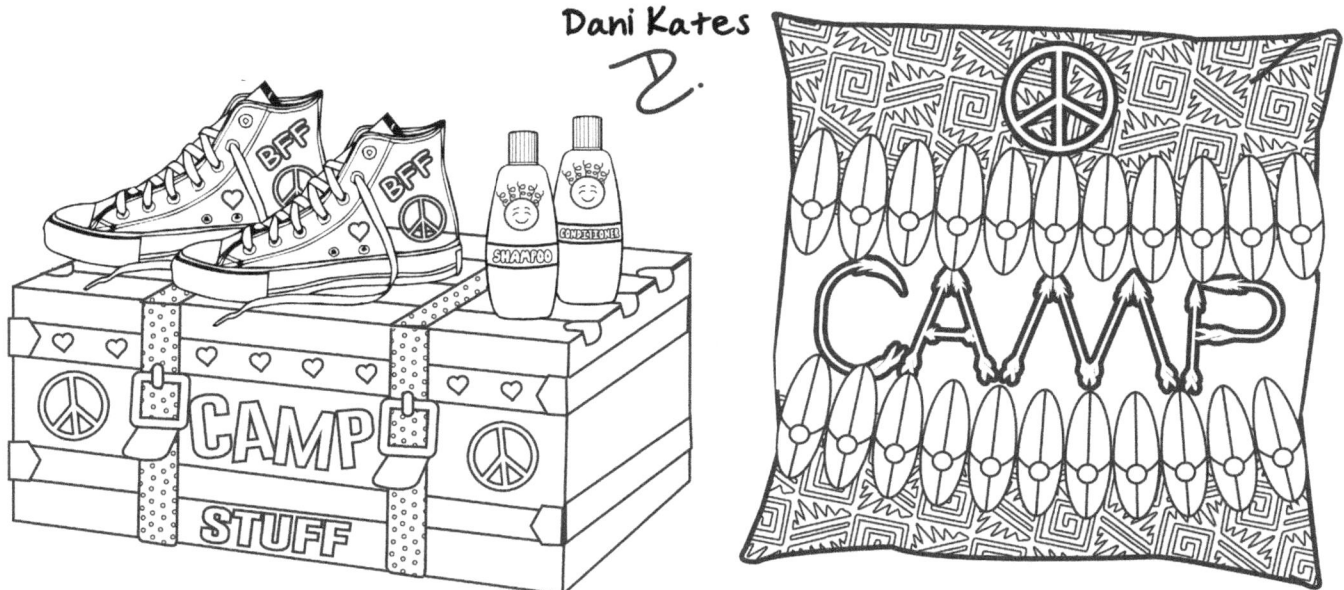

P.S. These are my two favorite pictures from the whole book!

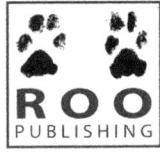

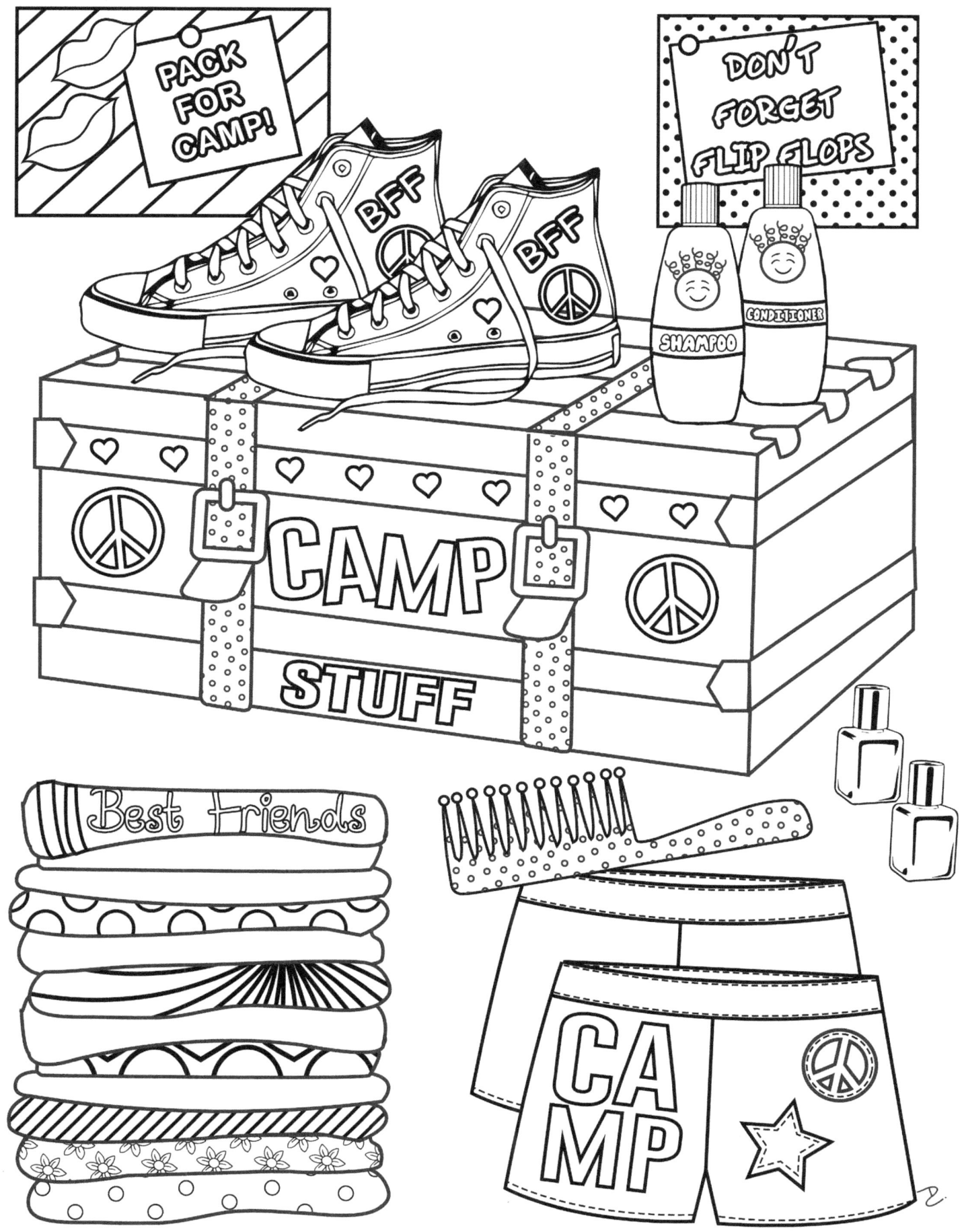

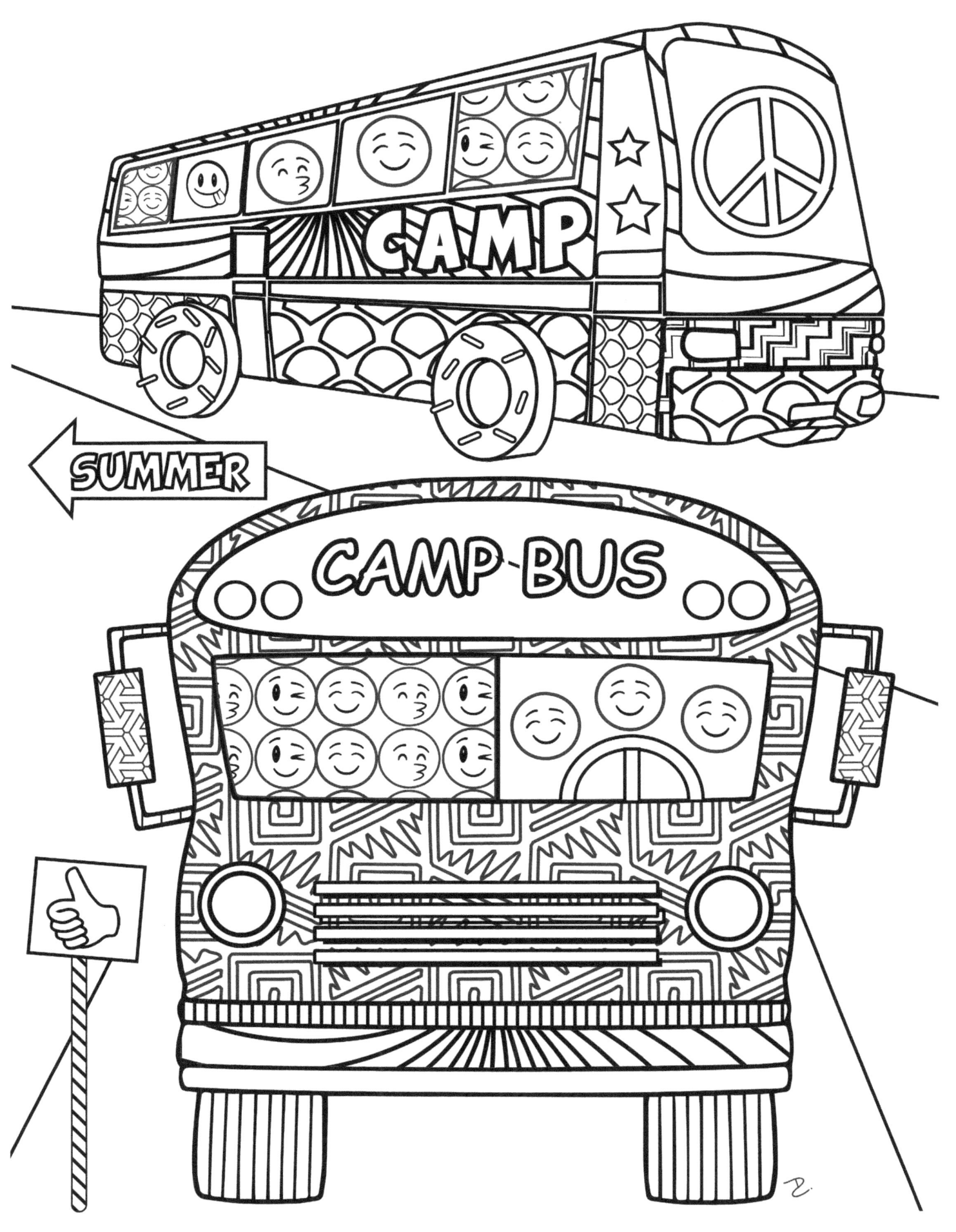

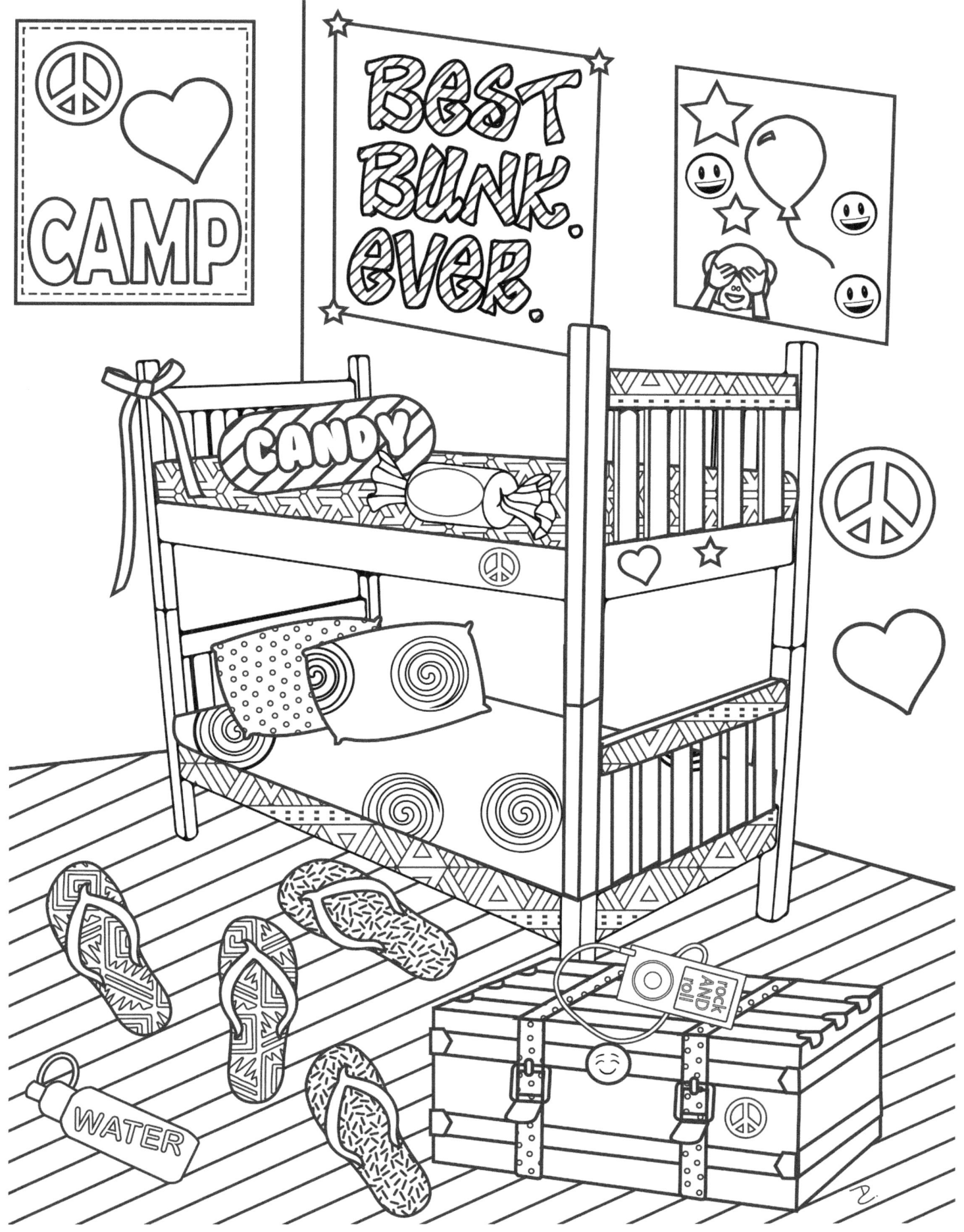

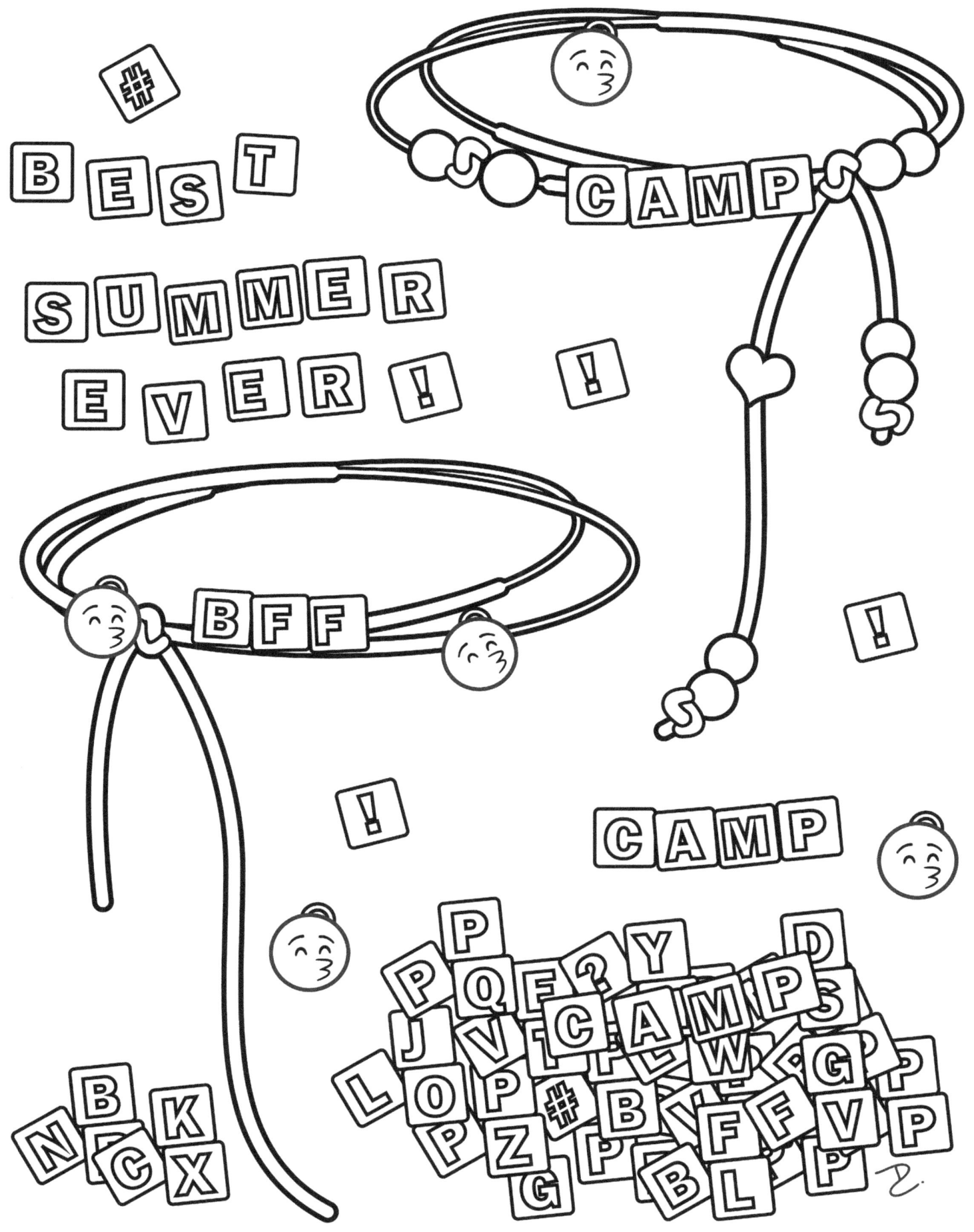

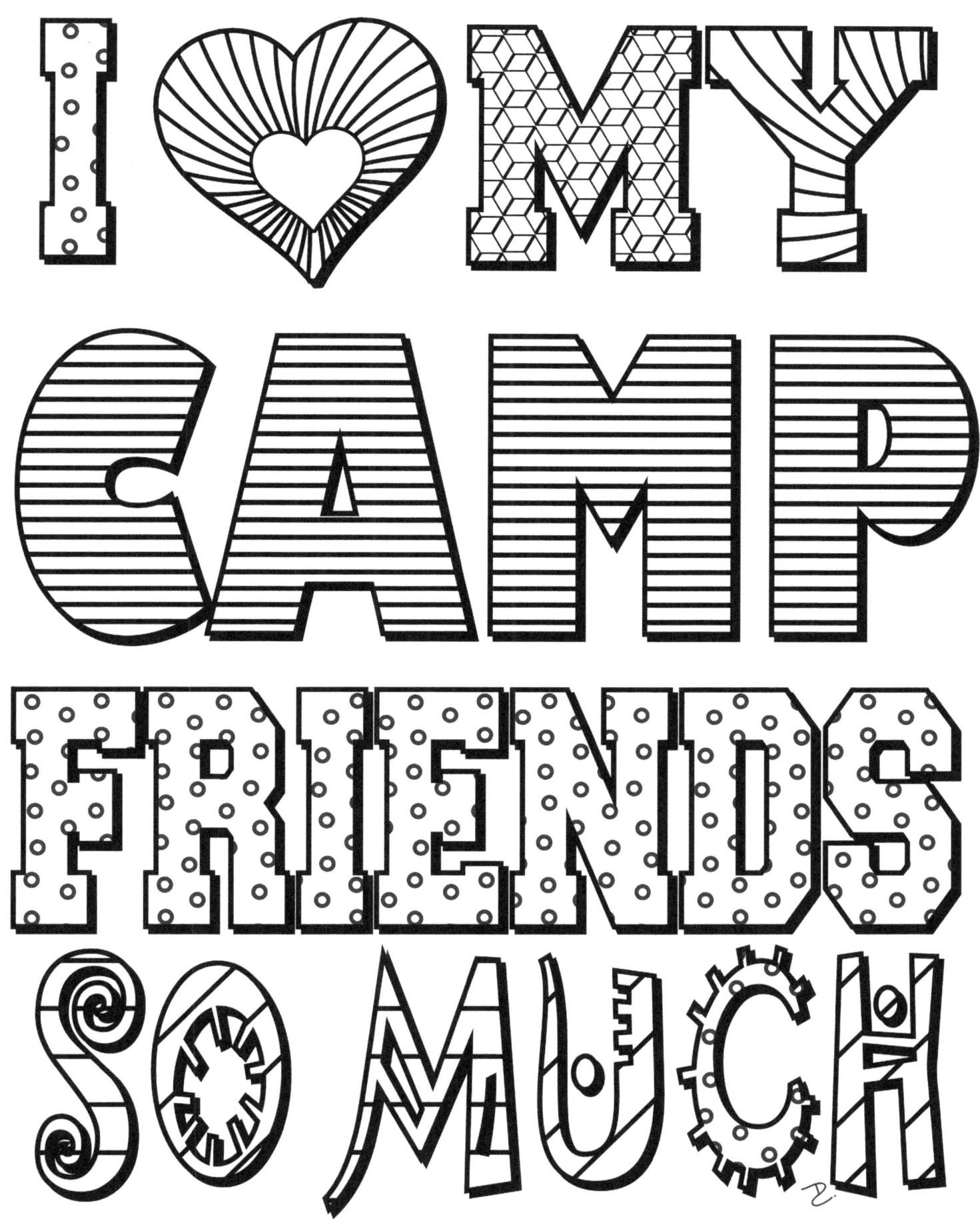

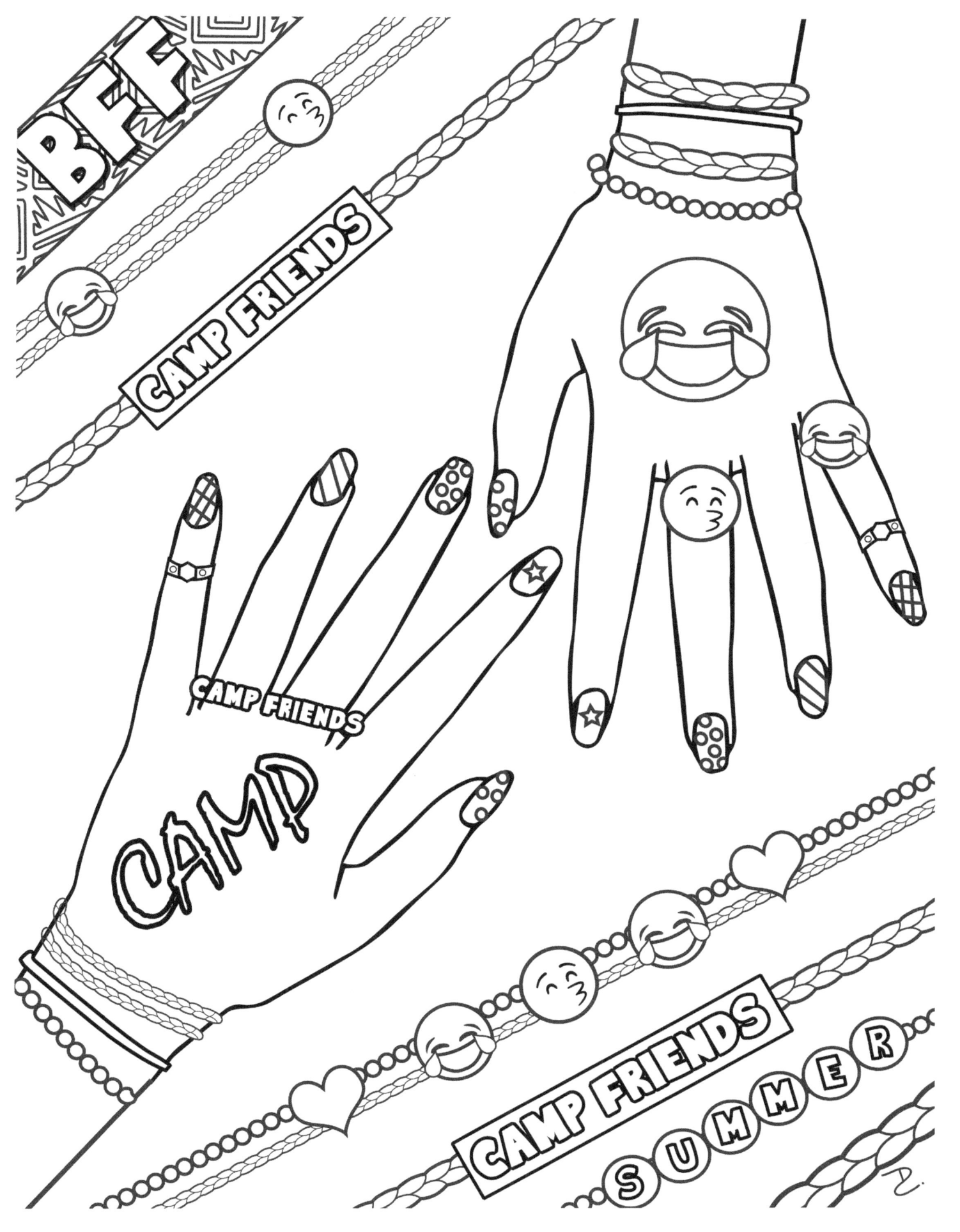

#CAMP
#SUMMER
#FRIENDS
#HAPPY
#LOVE
#MEMORIES

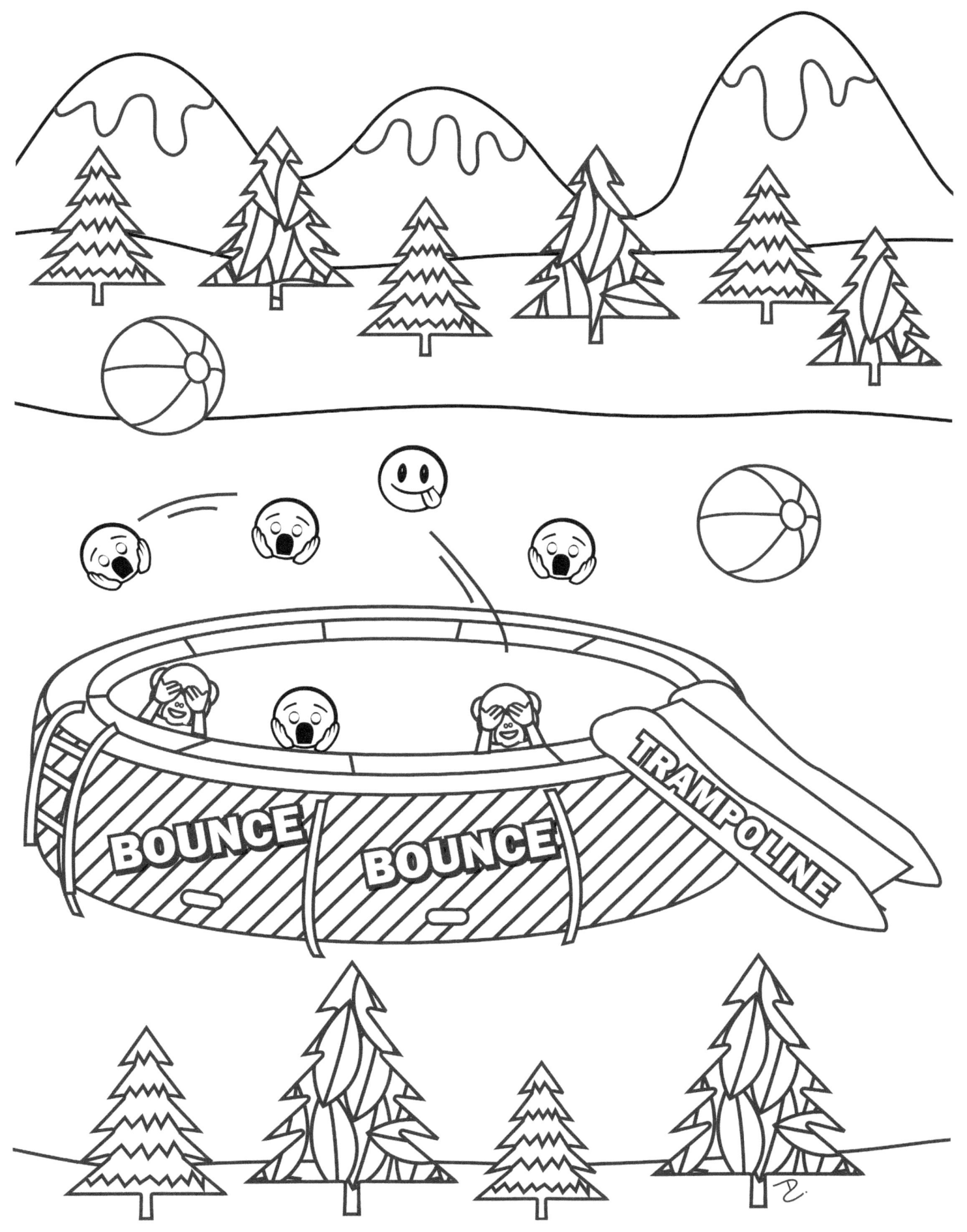

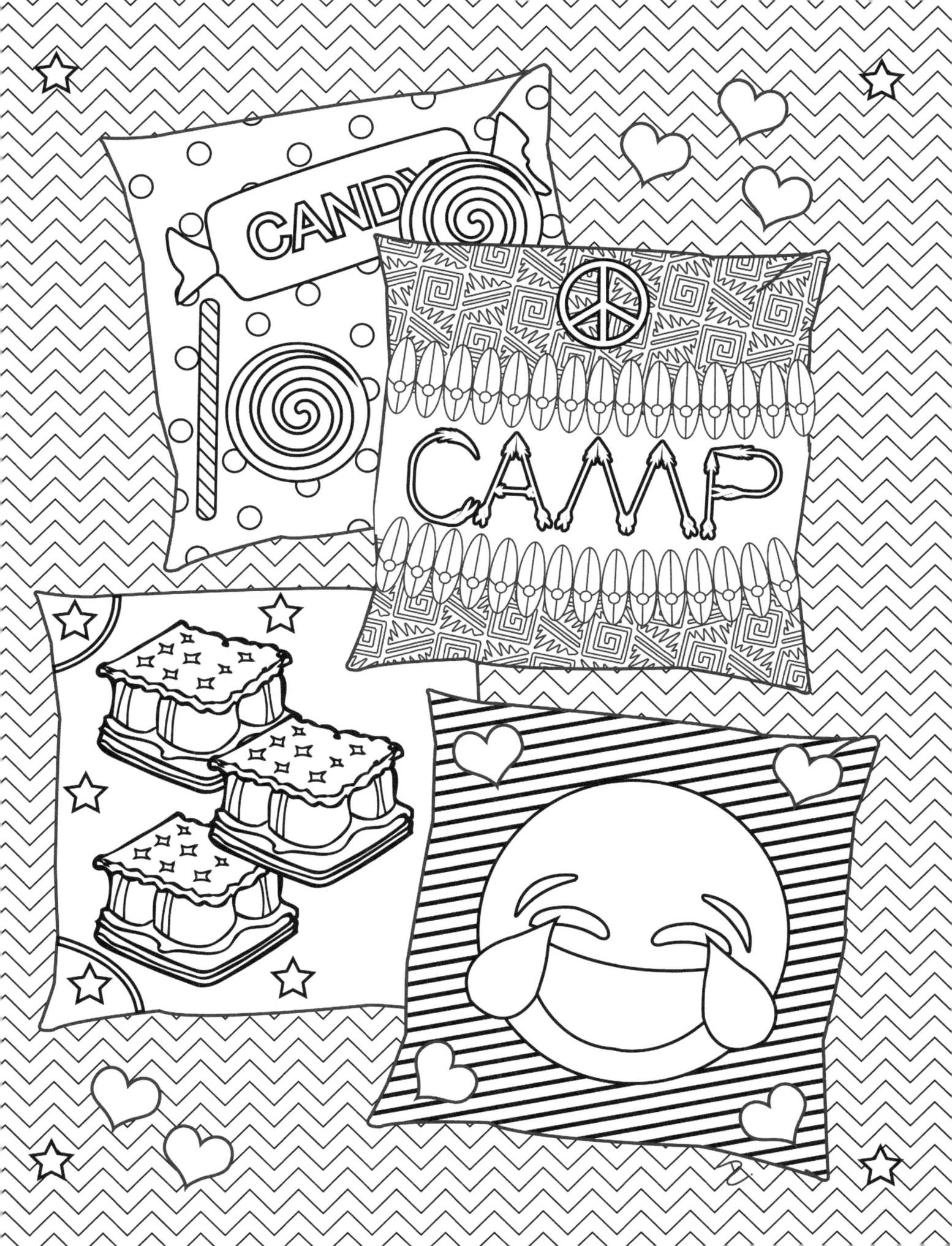

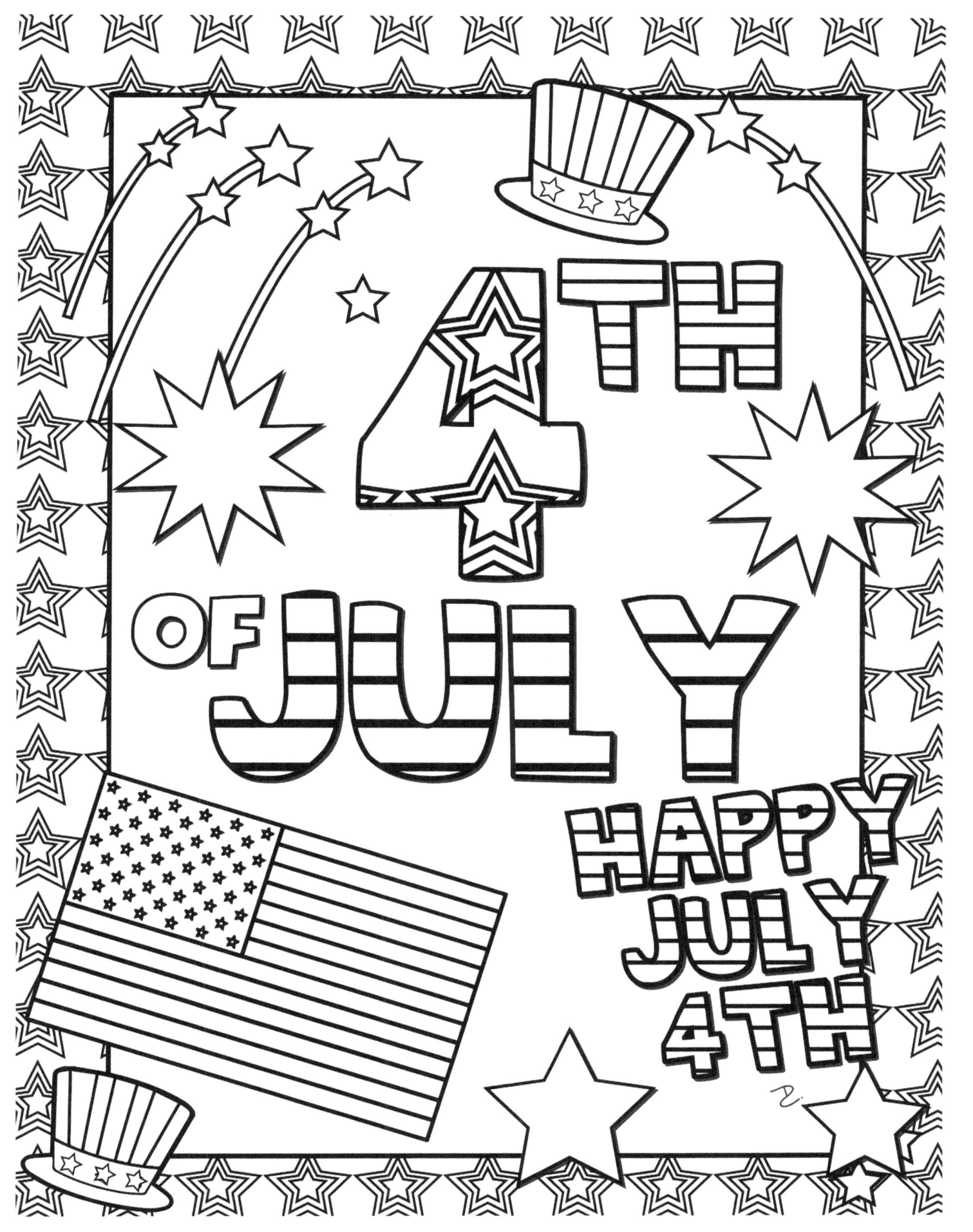

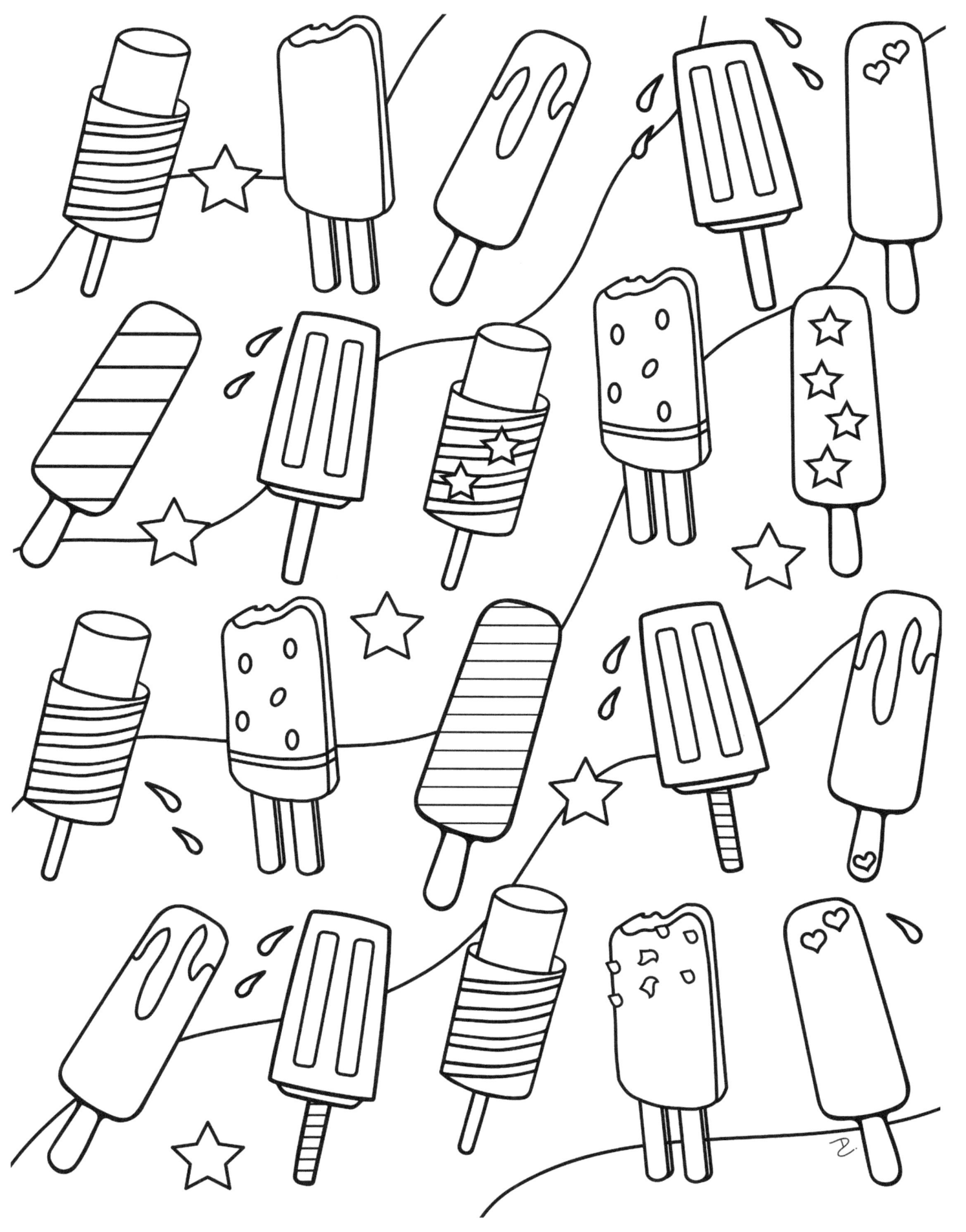

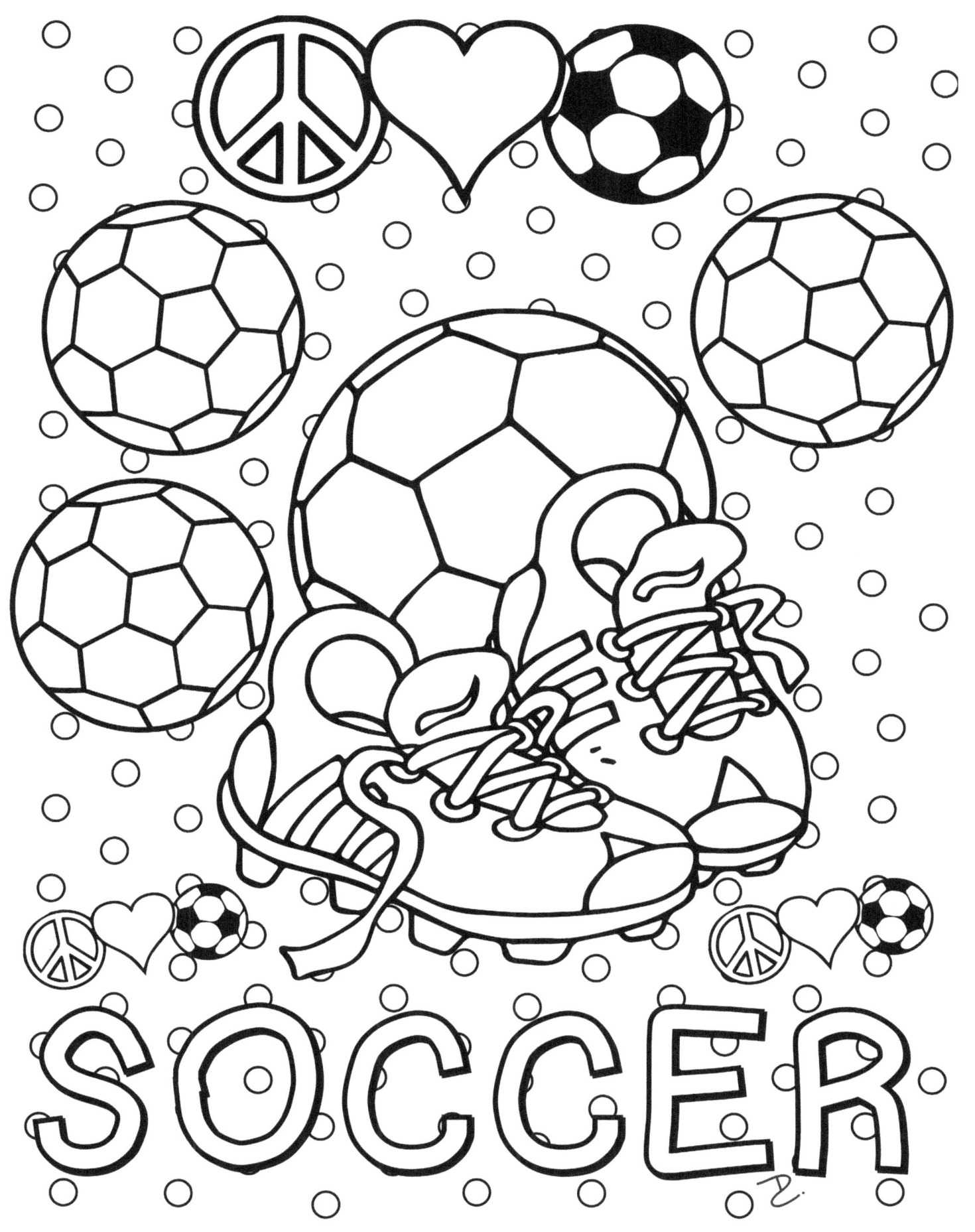

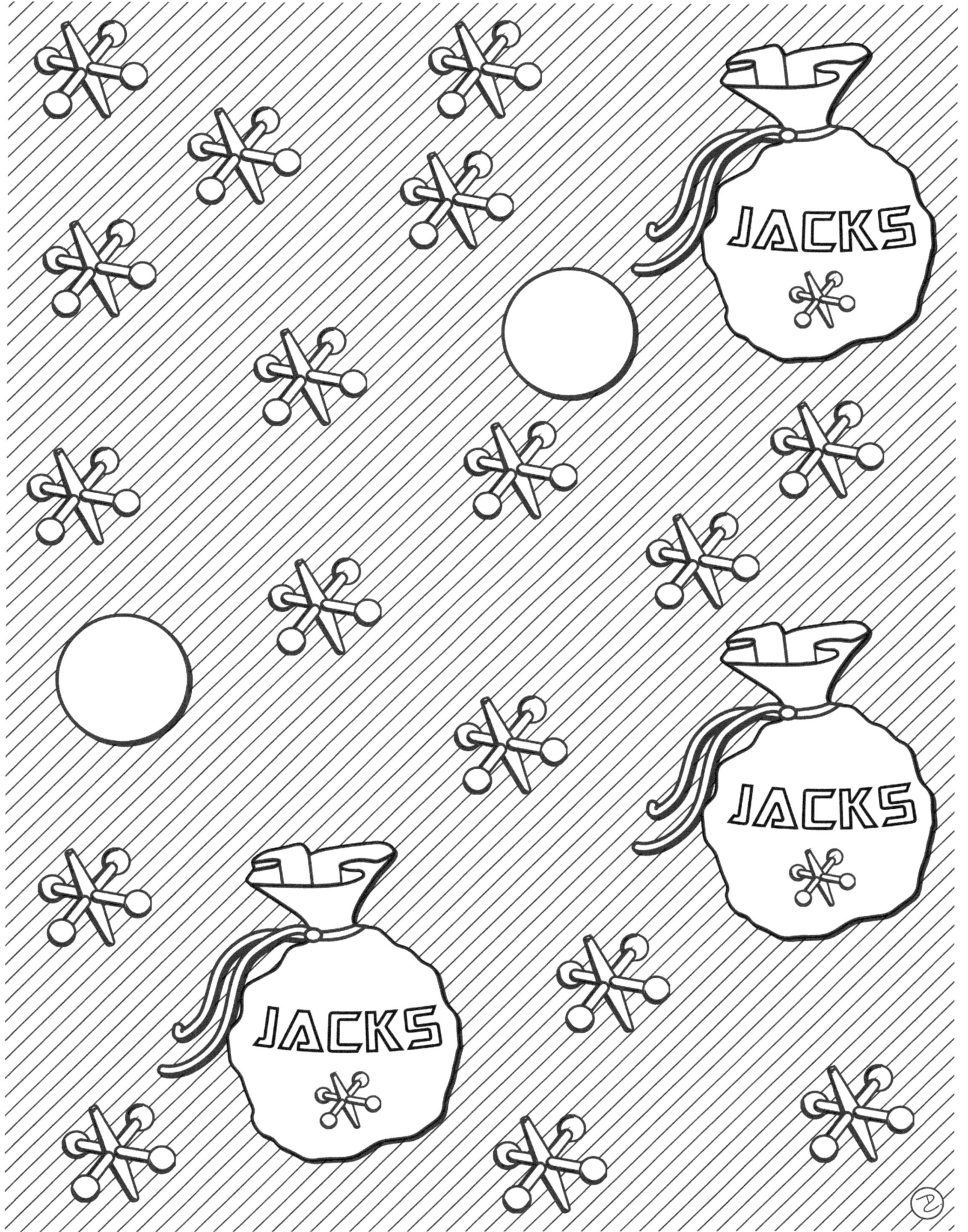

DEAR _____

CAMP IS _____

I REALLY ♡ _____

MY FAVORITE ACTIVITY
IS _____

CAN YOU PLEASE SEND
ME SOME _____?

I MISS YOU SO MUCH !!
LOVE, _____

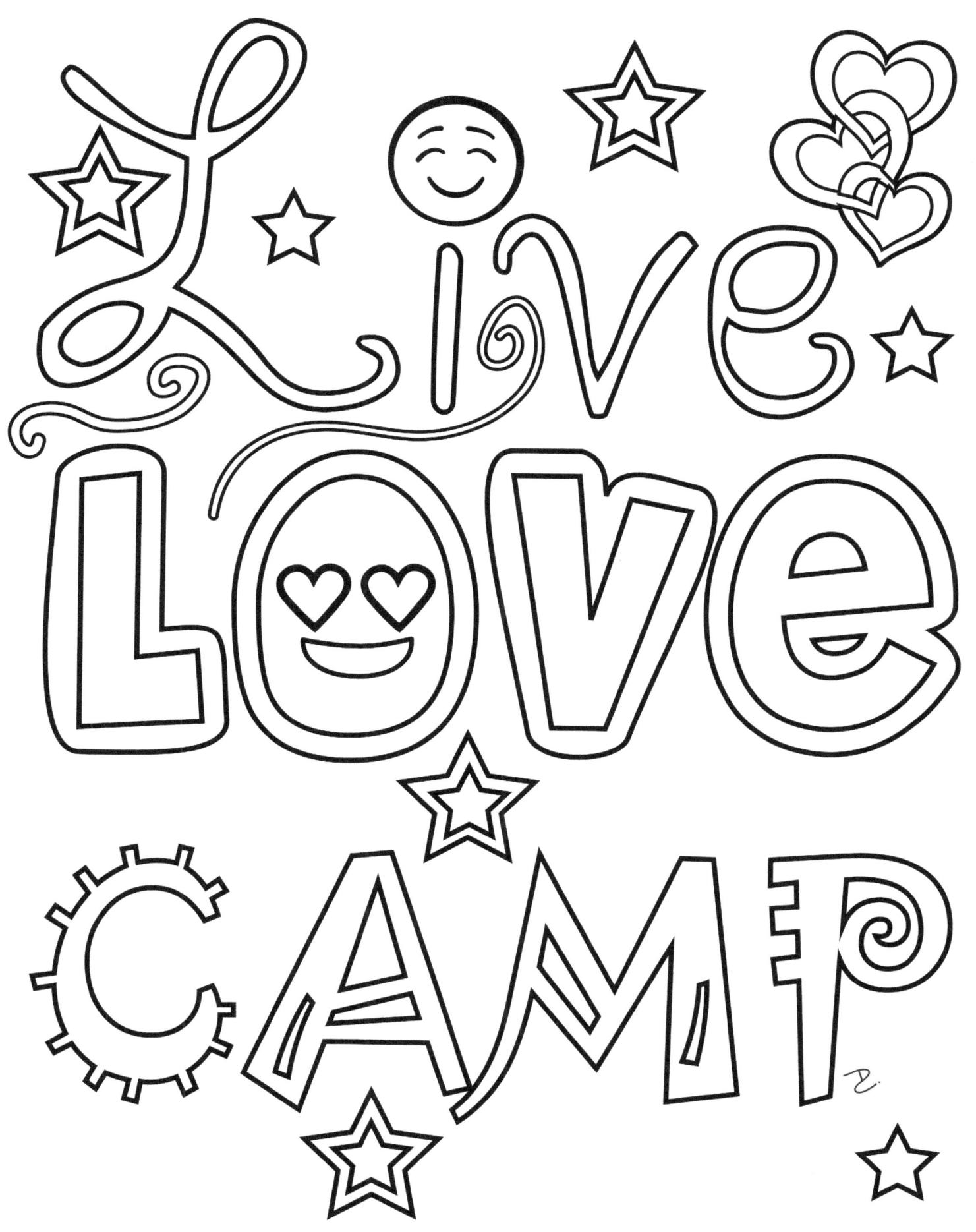

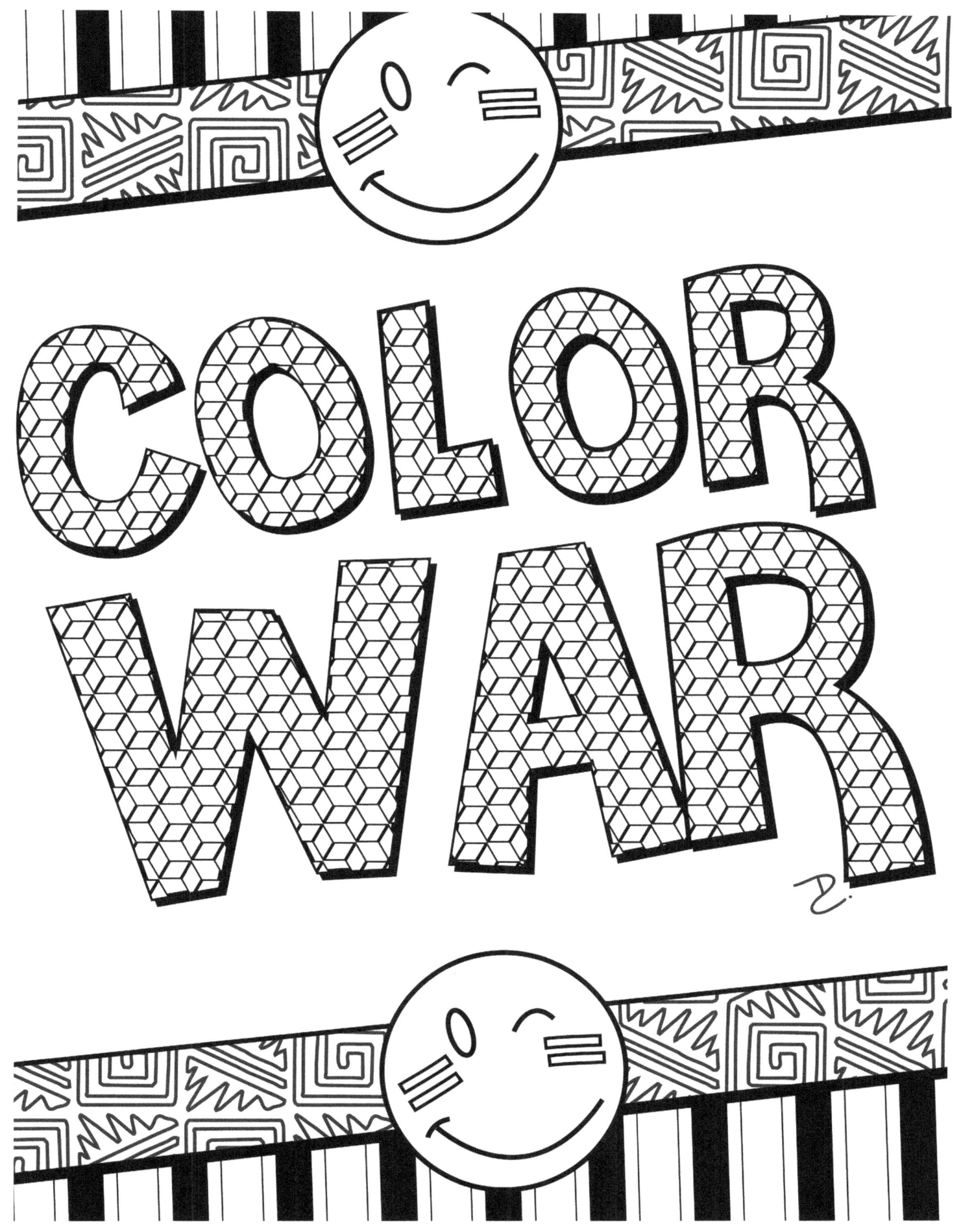

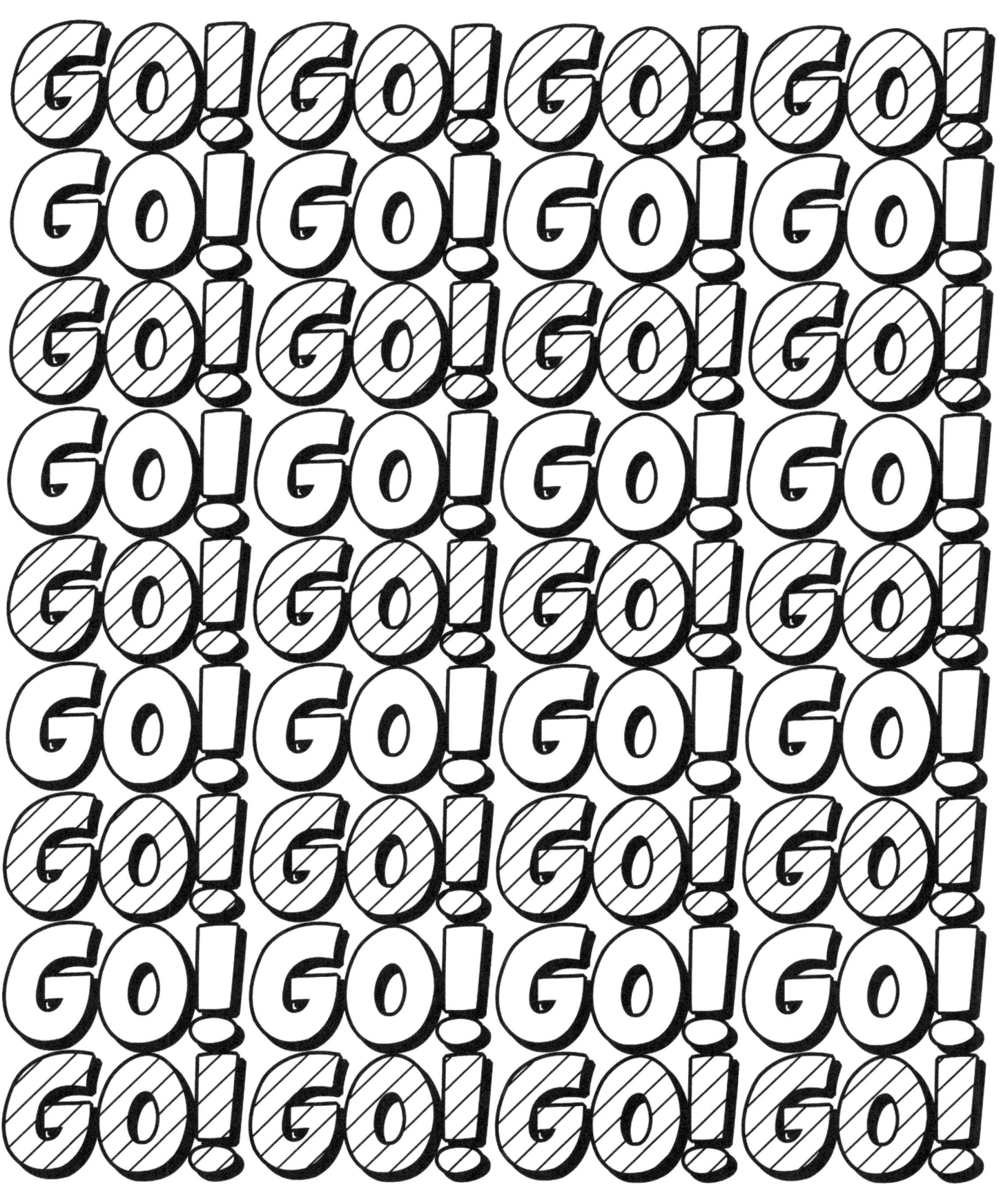

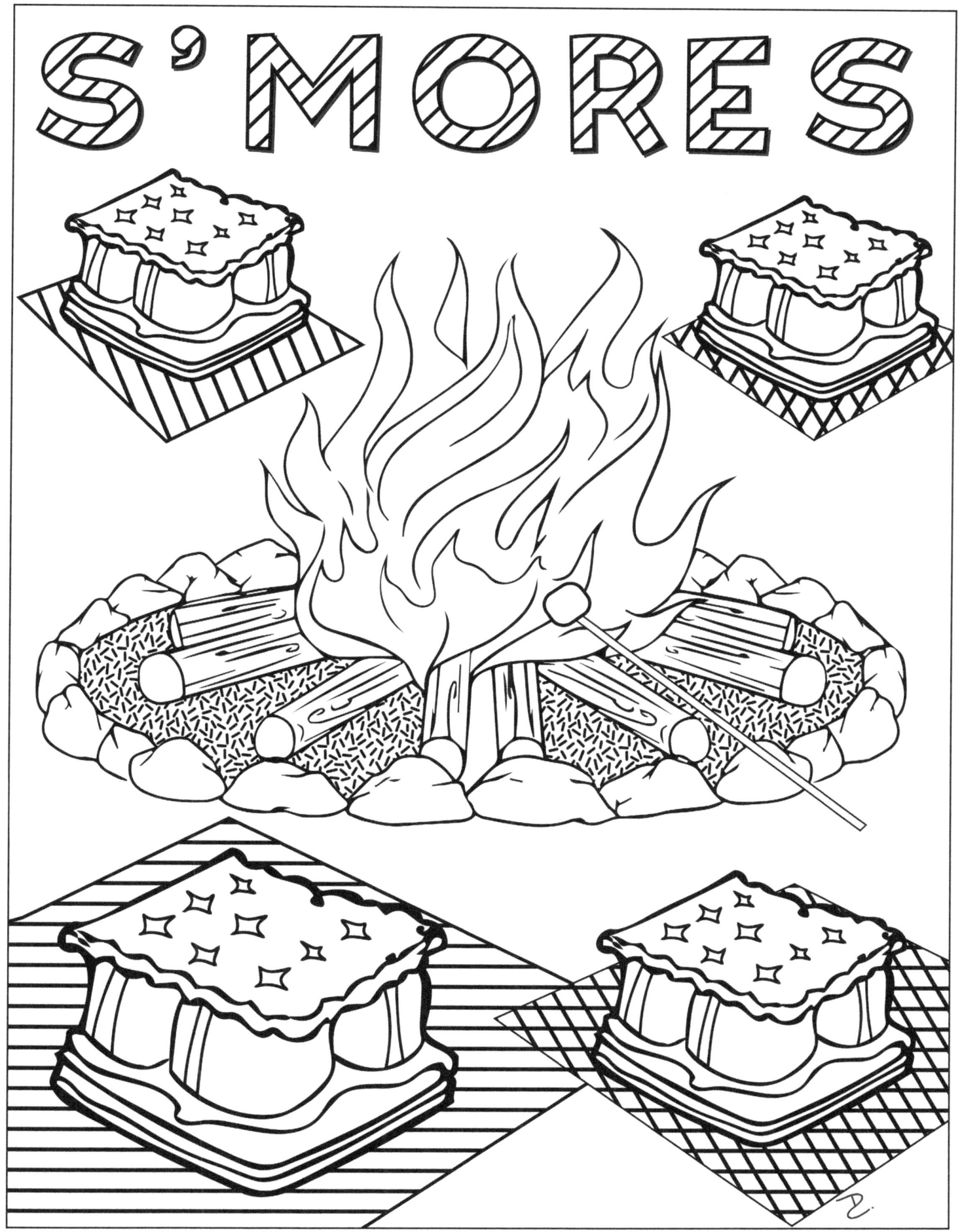

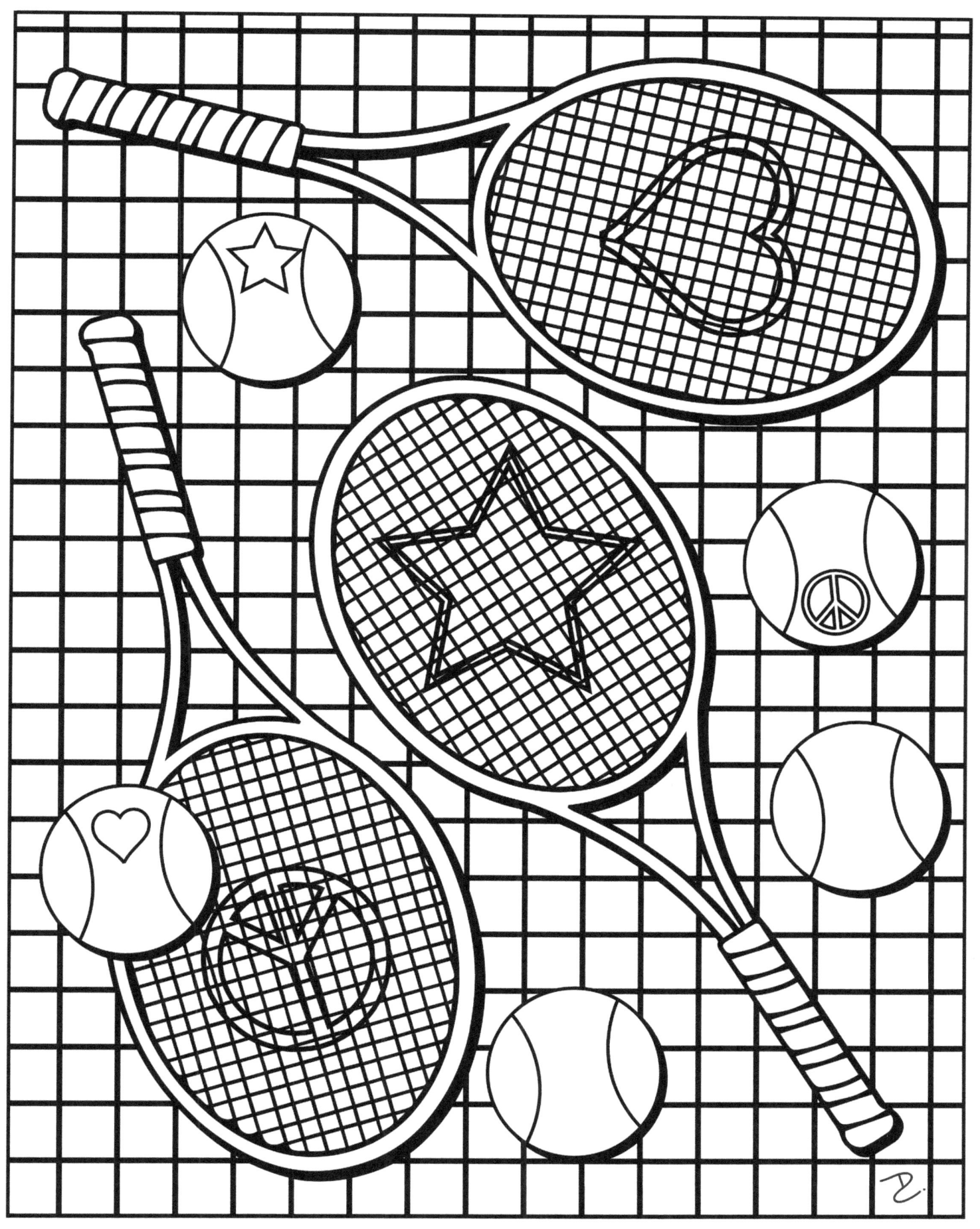

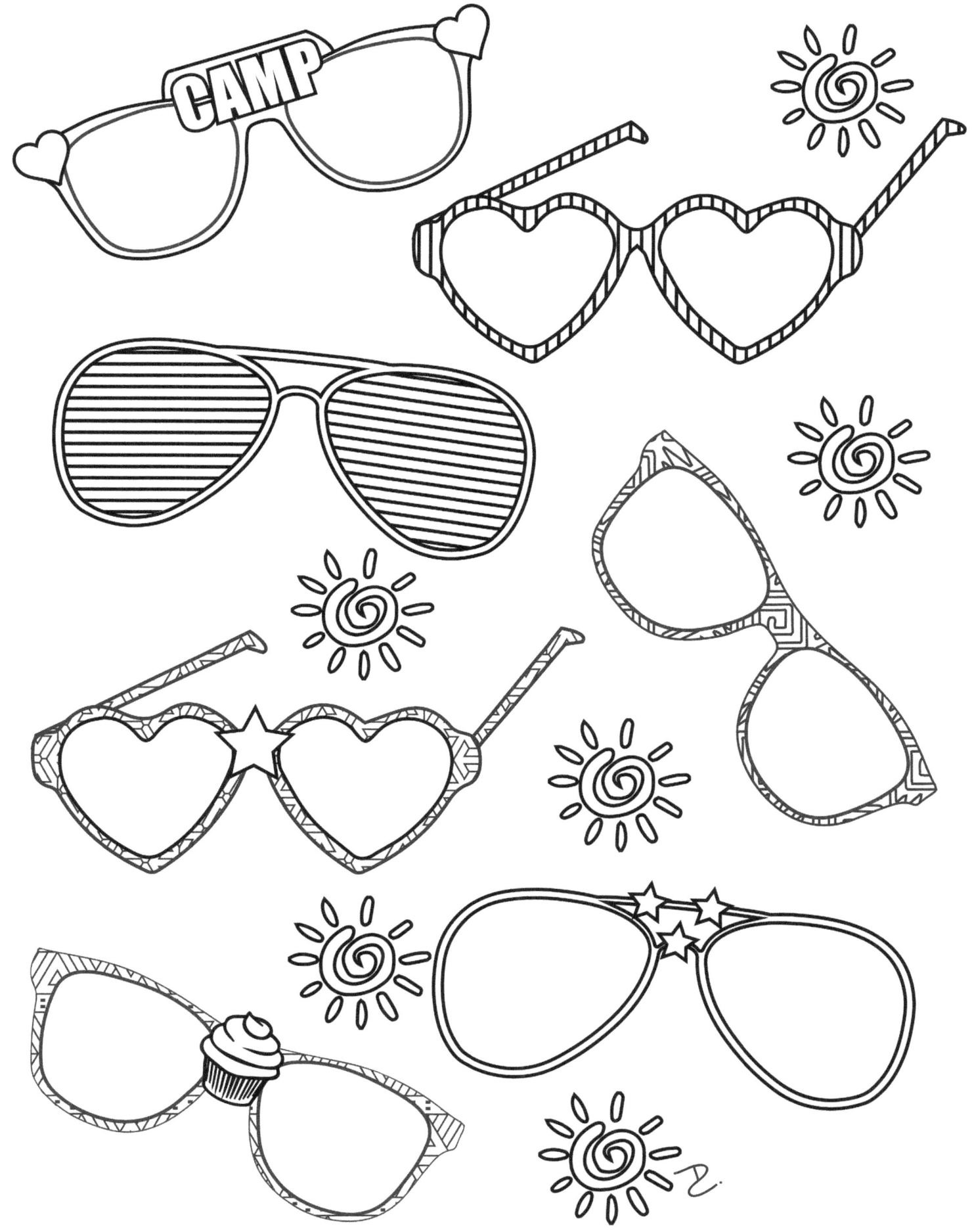

CAMP IS AWESOME

BUT I REALLY ♥ MISS YOU!

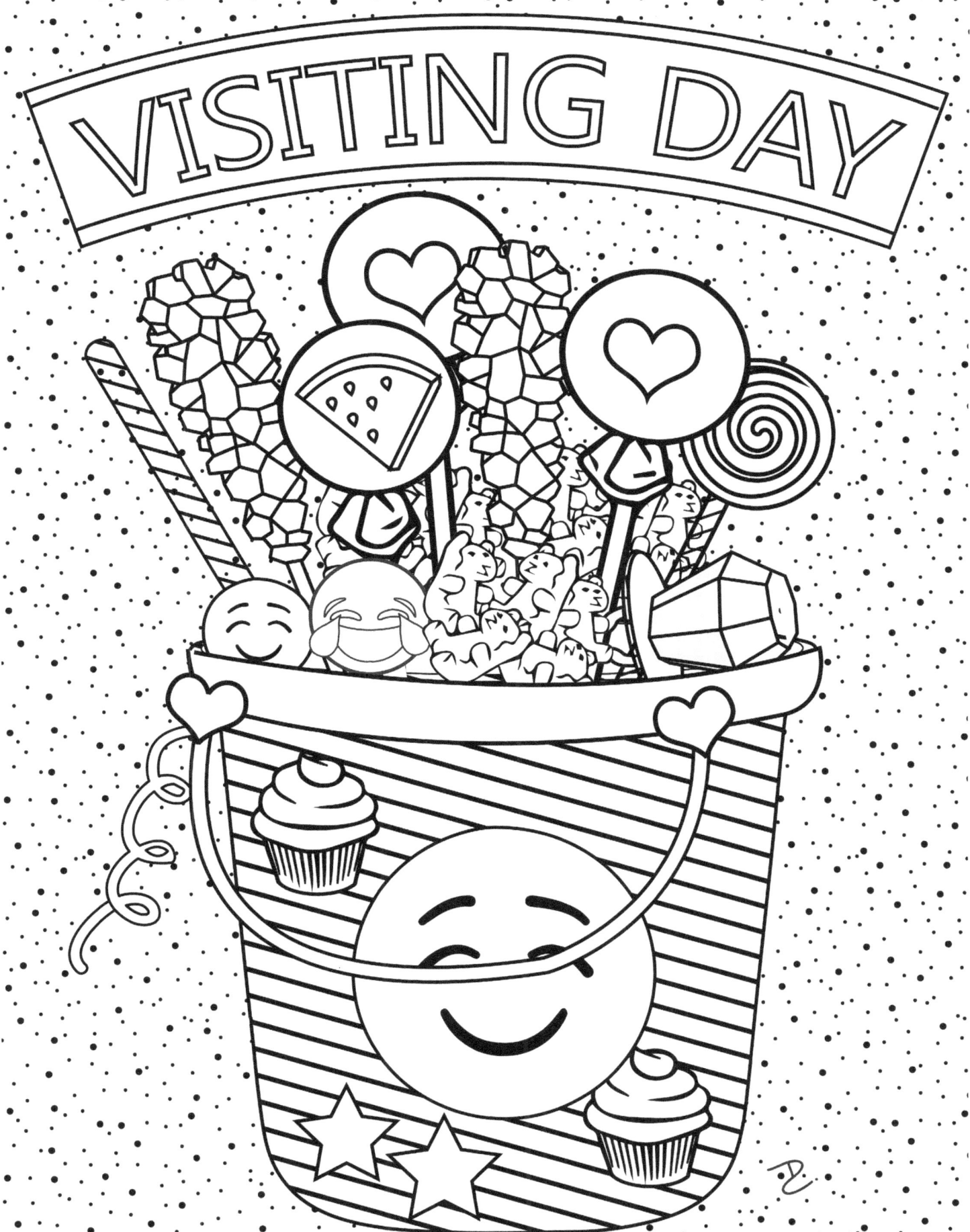

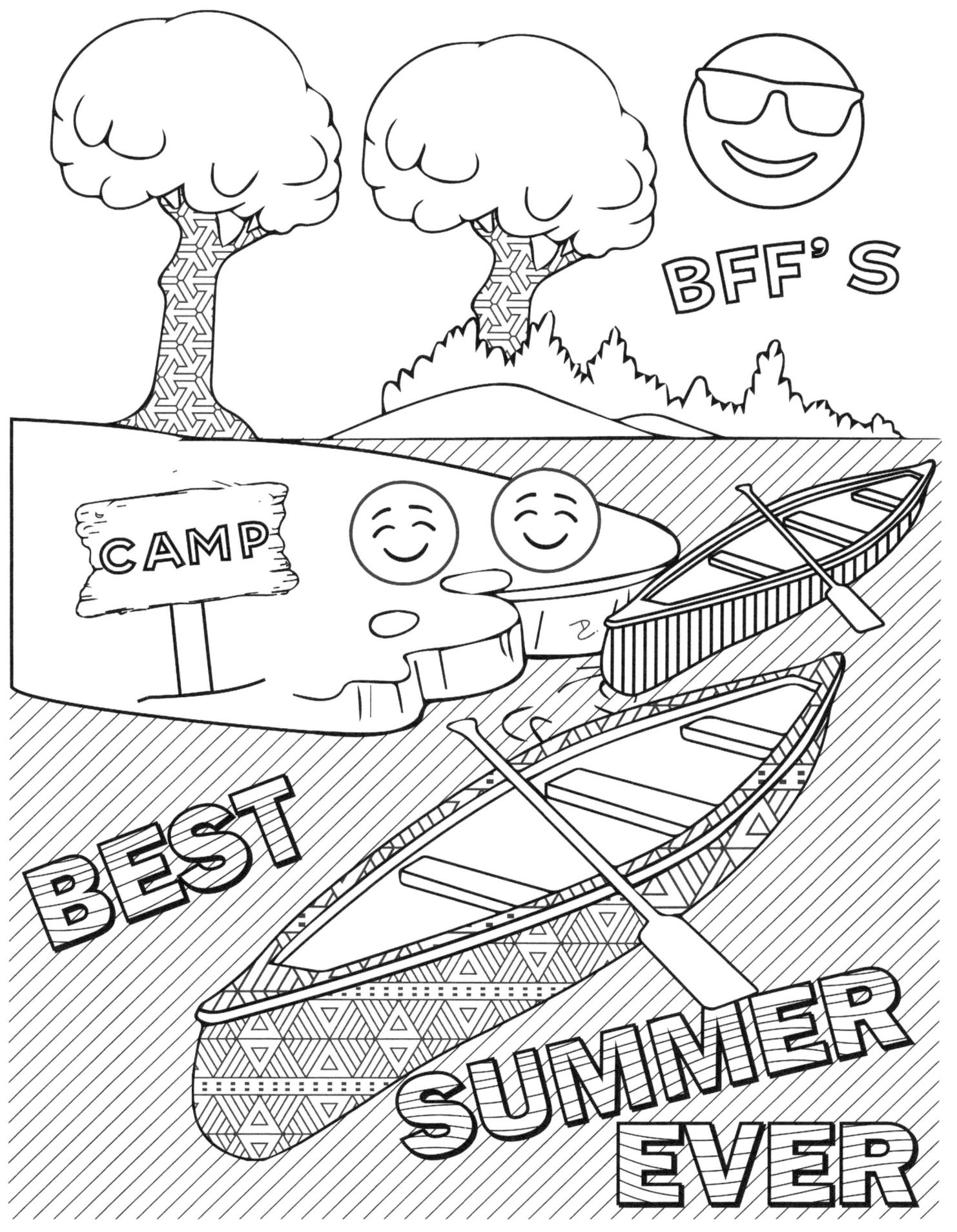

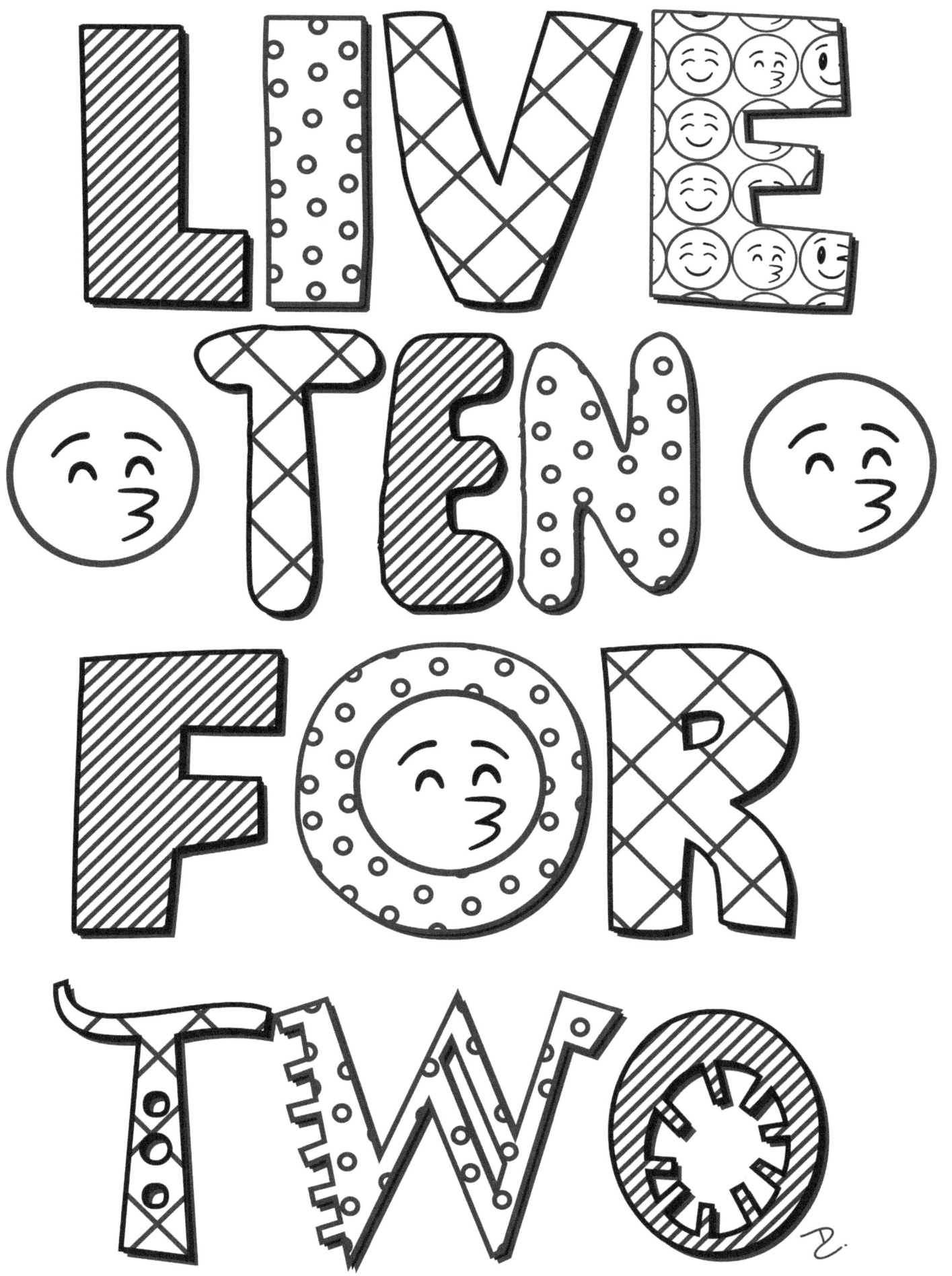